A MINDSET OF ABUNDANCE

A Guide To Creating An Abundant Mindset

OLAJUMOKE O. AKINTOLA

ISBN: 9798352204146

DEDICATION

This book is dedicated to my Dad Chief S.I Akintola as well as to all of my students, even those who have not yet discovered my contents.

CONTENTS

INTRODUCTION

It might be challenging to make our desires come true in the world we live in. It is simple to think that there are not enough resources available for everyone to enjoy. Some will try to convince you that the only way to access a higher quality of life is through advanced education or a college degree, but this is not the secret to abundance. You must change your perspective. Any person who has the chance to notice the plenty all around them will rapidly come to the realization that any objective is reachable. You only need to alter your perspective and broaden your capacity for receiving. You will discover how to alter your mentality in this manual. You can recognize and take advantage of all the wealth that is out there for you if you develop an abundant attitude.

For many people, abundance can imply different things. It's critical that you comprehend just what abundance means to you. Let's define abundance first. What does it look like for you to live an abundant life, exactly?

Mindsets come in two flavors

Abundance mindset and Scarcity mindset: Focusing on what we don't have and our limitations is more prevalent in the scarcity mindset. While maintaining the belief that there are sufficient resources for everyone to prosper, an abundance mindset focuses on generating opportunities.

A person with a scarcity mindset will become fixated on what is lacking in their life. When that happens, the mind becomes preoccupied with worrying and prevents us from achieving our goals in life.

Focusing on limitation and making hurdles appear can result in a scarcity mindset, which can seriously hinder our progress. You are not receptive to or aware of the abundance that is all around you when you limit yourself by your thoughts and behaviors.

It never suffices for a scarcity mind. The individual is of the opinion that a day will not be long enough to complete all of the tasks that can be completed in one. The scarcity mind is committed to recognizing what is unavailable, regardless of what it is.

The concept of abundance is represented on the reverse side of the medal. When we approach the world with that perspective, we see that there is plenty for everyone to benefit from. You put yourself first by letting go of unpleasant emotions like envy, jealousy, or self-pity. Your life changes when you go from victim to leader. Additionally, instead of concentrating on the limitations, you acknowledge the positive aspects of your life and make a conscious effort to attract more of what you desire. When someone has an abundance mindset, they get up with the intention of carving out some time for rest before making a list of all the things they can get done that day. The topic at hand is what is currently feasible or accessible.

STEP 1: ACQUIRE THE ABILITY TO RECEIVE

A strong conviction that we are unworthy of it is the main barrier preventing many of us from accepting the wealth that exists in our environment. Consider your response when someone compliments your talents or appearance. Do you often look for an explanation? Alternately, you might just switch the subject. When someone compliments them, those who have an abundant attitude are not hesitant to say "thank you." Start with a straightforward thank you if you want to start experiencing plenty.

Contrary Conduct: You Refuse to Request Assistance

You must be willing to receive if you want greater abundance in your life. And that involves asking for and receiving assistance.

You are sending a message to the universe that you

don't deserve aid from others if it is tough for you to say "yes" to someone who offers it. The same holds true if you find it difficult to ask for assistance. Many people are frequently surprised to learn that being independent in our lives can result in preventing the flow of prosperity.

The opposite of what you do is that you find compliments uncomfortable

In a way, accepting compliments is like asking for assistance. You are exhibiting that receiving is challenging for you if you find it tough to accept praises from others. You may experience more scarcity as a result. Consider your actions when someone commends your abilities.

Do you look for reasons why your performance isn't all that great?

Starting by expressing gratitude when someone sees your worth will help you become more receptive to receiving and attracting more income.

STEP 2: LOCATE YOUR PASSION

You must discover your area of passion if you want to live a life of abundance. We frequently strive to emulate others' actions just because they are successful. More abundance will come into your life as you align yourself more with what you love doing. You will stop the flow of abundance if you are attempting to be someone else because your intellect, not your heart, is where you should be. A person's success in something isn't a result of their actions, but rather who they are.

Alternate Action: Lay the Blame on Others

Perhaps you think that other people's actions rather than your own are to blame for many of the unpleasant circumstances you have encountered.

If so, it could be best for you to resolve the situation on your own. In essence, it is letting go of your independence and handing over total control of your life to someone else or some other external force. You become helpless and unable to alter your circumstances when you relinquish your control. The capacity to accept responsibility and take action to improve one's circumstances is one of the most typical behaviors among those with an abundance mindset. You cannot feel empowered to take action to improve your life if you do not accept responsibility for your actions.

STEP 3: FEEL HOWEVER YOU WANT TO

While knowing what you want is vital, feeling what you want is much more crucial. You'll attract what you desire into your life more often if you align yourself with the positive feelings it makes you feel.

Contrary Action: You Feel Envious of Others

We frequently experience feelings of envy when we adopt a scarcity mindset. It's common for us to discover ourselves wishing we could have what someone else has while observing them. One of the frequent questions you might have is "Why does everyone else have what they want but not me?" Due to the way envy makes us think about our lack of something, it draws lack. Additionally, it can damage friendships and family ties and cause animosity for certain people.

STEP 4: TAKE STOCK OF YOUR RESOURCES

Recognizing how rich your life already is a straightforward step towards abundance. Spend some time reflecting on your blessings. Perhaps it is your physical well-being, the people you care about, your coworkers, your abilities, or the everyday beauty of nature. Your ability to draw good things into your life increases as you put more of your mind in a state of appreciation and recognition. You'll come to see how bountiful your life is and how everything you require is right in front of you.

The opposite of this is to pay attention to the gaps

Placing all of our focus and effort on what is lacking in our lives is a common error we make when we have a scarcity mindset. Individuals who lead prosperous lives, on the other hand, are accustomed to focusing their concentration on the things they wish to manifest. You can create a clear picture of what you want by changing the focus of your thoughts to be more in line with your goals. When you are clear about what you want as opposed to what you know you don't want, it is simpler to find what you are looking for. Do you frequently make a list of what you believe to be lacking from your life? Do you ever question why something isn't available to you? Do you tend to be the type of person that is usually thinking about how to get more?

A different approach would be to dwell on the past

To constantly ponder about the past is to waste a lot of your valuable time on things that are no longer important. You don't have enough energy as a result of that habit to achieve your goals. You must decide now whether or not to embrace your history and shift your attention back to what you can do right now to feel better. Consider what action you can do immediately to help you access more abundance if you want to live a more fulfilling life. What positive things are happening in your life right now? People who have an abundance mindset don't put off enjoying a good life because they are waiting for something they will acquire later. They discover happiness in the present.

STEP 5: COMPLETE SIMPLE TASKS

It takes time to become prosperous. The vast majority of people who enjoy bountiful lives will tell you that they work hard every day to maintain it. They carry out tiny tasks every day that are in line with their goals for their lives. You could make little daily contributions into a savings account, for instance, if you wanted more money. By the end of the year, it will have grown significantly. If, however, you desire more love in your life, begin by loving yourself. Make it a point to bring to mind one aspect of yourself each day that you appreciate.

Use of the Words "Don't" or "Can't" Frequently

Our choice of words reveals a lot about our thinking. The words "can't," "won't," or "don't" are frequently used by someone with a scarcity mindset. These comments have a propensity to feed the deep-seated perception that we lack sufficient resources and lack the ability to achieve our life goals. Be mindful of your language as you transition to a more wealthy existence.

Recognize when you are using language that creates a limiting mindset and reframe it so that it gives you the power to take action.

All people on this planet have the ability to live prosperous lives; it just relies on their attitude. By putting the above advice into practice, you will be better able to tap into the wealth around you and make the life you want a reality.

Once you are completely aware of your thoughts and have the ability to shift from limiting ideas and a scarcity-based mindset to one that is focused on abundance, you will discover an abundant, joyful, and fulfilled existence. You should be aware that anyone may successfully access an abundance mindset and accomplish everything they truly desire and feel they deserve.

ABOUT THE AUTHOR

Olajumoke O. Akintola is a goal oriented, tireless worker who sees possibilities in all things regardless of the situation. She believes regardless of how many times you fall, try rising again.

What makes this book unique is that you will be able to recognize and take advantage of all the wealth that is out there for you if you develop an abundant attitude.

www.ingramcontent.com/pod-product-compliance
Lightning Source LLC
LaVergne TN
LVHW052116160826
845678LV00015B/3587

* 9 7 9 8 3 5 2 2 0 4 1 4 6 *